THINKING OF YOU

you're my
SWEET

Cards That Wow

WITH Sizzix

TECHNIQUES AND IDEAS FOR USING DIE-CUTTING AND EMBOSSING MACHINES

Creative Publishing

Ellison

EQUIPMENT, INC.
25862 COMMERCENTRE
DRIVE
LAKE FOREST, CA 92630
sizzix.com
Ellison® & Sizzix®
are trademarks of
Ellison Educational
Equipment, Inc.
©2015 Ellison

Customer Service Hours
6:30 a.m. to 4:00 p.m.,
Pacific Time,
Monday through Friday

By Phone
877.355.4766
(Toll Free in the USA)
949.598.8821
(Outside of the USA)

Stephanie Barnard® and
The Stamps of Life™ are
trademarks of Stephanie
Barnard Designs Inc.

Tim Holtz® is a trademark
of Tim Holtz LLC.

First published in the United States
of America in 2015
by Creative Publishing international,
a member of
Quarto Publishing Group USA Inc.
400 First Avenue North, Suite 400
Minneapolis, MN 55401
Telephone: 1-800-328-3895
www.creativepub.com

10 9 8 7 6 5 4 3 2 1
ISBN: 978-1-58923-884-8

W PRESS

215 Historic 25th Street,
Ogden, Utah 84401

Cover Design: Mattie Wells
Design Production: Lisa Ballard
Photographer: Ryne Hazen, Hazen Photography
Copy Editor: Cynthia Levens

Kristin Highberg

FOREWORD

What makes a great card?

I am sure that no two cardmakers would answer that question the same—just as no two cards are the same. This uniqueness is what we celebrate and imaginatively create with our award-winning Sizzix® machines and countless complementary designs.

In her fabulous, inspiration-filled book, *Cards That Wow*, Stephanie Barnard takes the wow factor to a whole new level. Stephanie has created cards that are easy to make and, yet, very special to give. Never again will you need to worry about finding the perfect inspiration to show how much you care...because it's all right here!

So the next time you need to add a little pizzazz or want some personalization that really pops, just go ahead and have another look through this amazing book...you never know what you may dream up!

Happy Crafting,

Kristin Highberg

Chief Executive Officer
Ellison/Sizzix

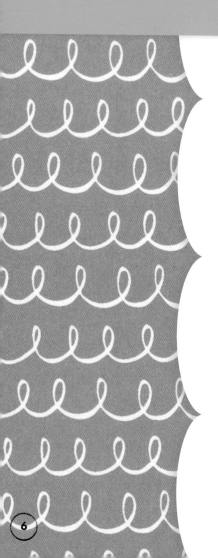

Contents

PAGE
66 Holidays

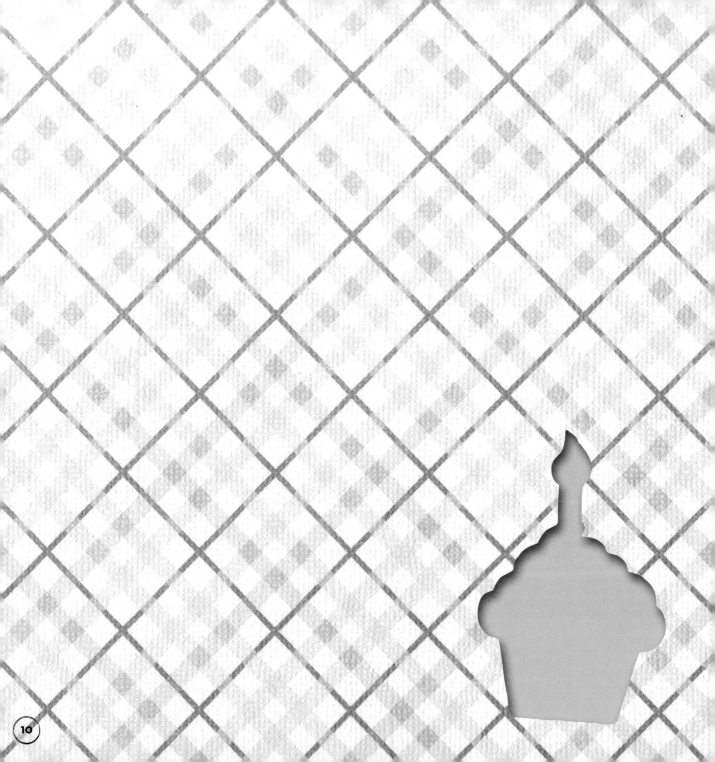

How-To
instructions

Welcome

to the World of Sizzix®, where creativity abounds! Our product line of machines, dies, and accessories delivers unlimited opportunities to create a variety of projects to express your creativity and enhance your life.

This book is filled with projects that focus on card design. Not only will you see ideas for greeting cards, holiday cards, and tags, you will also find inspiration for the perfect thank you cards. We are sharing ideas that will help you personalize your cards in countless ways, while making use of the colorful papers and embellishments we all love.

Many of the cards in this book have interesting folds, movement and display capabilities, and are all created using Sizzix® dies! Imagine the possibilities of combining Sizzix® dies and stamps with your favorite papers and embellishments. **Explore and have fun!**

Ideas from the Experts

Beginning Crafters Welcome!

These beautifully crafted cards have been created by experienced and talented designers, but do not worry—the projects in this book can be embraced by crafters at all levels. Whether you replicate a card exactly, use a particular project as a jumping off place, or just use the volume as ingredients for a future creative recipe, you are certain to find the pages that follow to be an inspirational feast! Our team worked their magic using cardstock, patterned papers, stamps, and embellishments.

Lay of the Land

Rather than taking you through each project step-by-step, *Cards That Wow* with Sizzix® is an idea book that will spark your creative fire. Each project photo is accompanied by a list of dies and stamps used as well as tips and tricks to help you make the project yourself. When a die is not listed for the card base, a card base can easily be created using an 8½ x 11 inch (A4 size) piece of cardstock cut in half (either way) and then folded. This creates a standard A2 size card when folded (4¼ x 5½ inches).

Feel free to express your own creativity by selecting similar or different colors/patterns and embellishments. Use this book as a springboard for your creations.

Die-Cutting Basics

Are you new to die cutting and embossing? You're going to love it! Our machines, dies, and embossing folders are easy to use—you will be hooked! The creative possibilities are truly endless and talk about a time saver! Why spend ages cutting out multiple pieces?

You can die cut multiples in a minute or two using your Big Shot™ Machine. You are, also, going to love the variety of materials you can cut. Our steel-rule dies cut materials like fabric, leather, magnetic sheets, burlap, vinyl, foam, felt, compressed sponge, matboard, craft metal, and more. Almost anything that is up to ⅛ inch (3 mm) thick our machines can cut. Our Framelits dies can cut cardstock, vellum, patterned paper, wool felt, and other thinner items.

Enjoy our book's inspiration! We are sure it will inspire you to create incredible Cards That Wow!

Getting Started

**Making a Basic Sizzix®
Sandwich using Wafer-Thin,
Chemically-Etched Dies**

Place material to be die cut on Cutting Pad. Place die over material and align. Place another Cutting Pad over the die and material to create a "sandwich." Place sandwich on Extended Multipurpose Platform and slide the Platform into the opening of the machine. Note the rotation of the handle and continue to rotate it in the same direction until the sandwich has passed through the opening of the rollers. Remove the sandwich from the machine. Your die-cut shape is ready to use!

Using Framelits™, Thinlits™ or other Wafer-Thin Dies

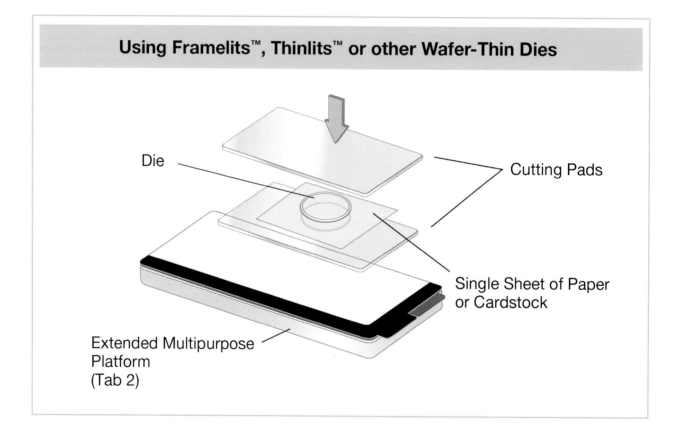

Die

Cutting Pads

Single Sheet of Paper or Cardstock

Extended Multipurpose Platform (Tab 2)

MACHINES

Big Shot™ | BIGkick™

This versatile die-cutting machine really is the hub of any crafter's universe. As a portable roller machine, it easily cuts and embosses many different materials. Create your own one-of-a-kind cards, invitations, scrapbook pages, home décor, fashion, altered art, quilting, and much more!

Big Shot™ Pro

For the crafter who wants it all, comes the pro-strength machine that does it all. From our embossing folders to our smallest dies to our biggest 12 inch Bigz™ Pro dies, the Big Shot Pro machine works with any Sizzix® die or embossing folder to create an amazing assortment of craft shapes.

Vagabond™

Inspired by Tim Holtz®, the Vagabond machine easily opens up to reveal a portable yet powerful machine that takes you to imaginative new places. Upon closer examination, the Vagabond impresses with its uncanny ability to effortlessly cut and emboss many different materials and thicknesses.

Texture Boutique™

Resembling an ornate purse with a beaded handle, this amazing embossing machine is perfect for creating cards for any occasion, transforming ordinary cardstock and other thin materials into elegant embossed art.

SophistiCut™

With a stylish purse design and refined die-cutting capabilities, the SophistiCut creates many charming shapes using small, medium, and border-sized Sizzix Originals™ dies. Experience appliqué, home décor, fashion, jewelry, cardmaking, and more in pure elegance.

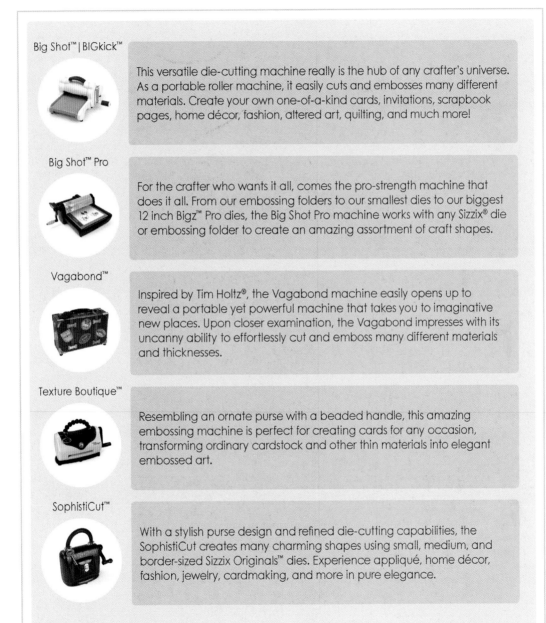

TECHNOLOGY

steel-rule

Look out for Bigz™, Originals™, On The Edge™, and Movers & Shapers™ dies. These will cut a wide range of materials, making them perfect for papercrafting, home décor, quilting, and more!

Cuts:
- cardstock
- felt
- fabric
- foam
- magnet
- leather
- craft aluminum
- chipboard
- metallic foil
- and much more!

wafer-thin

Our Framelits™ and Thinlits™ dies are perfect for layering and cutting apertures and a whole host of intricate shapes that will make your papercrafting really stand out from the crowd!

Cuts:
- cardstock
- paper
- metallic foil
- vellum

chemically-etched

Check out our Sizzlits® and Embosslits™. Designed to cut a single sheet of cardstock, Sizzlits create fabulous little shapes that make a great big difference with your papercrafting. Go one step further with Embosslits – these clever little dies cut AND emboss for some very impressive results!

Cuts:
- cardstock
- paper
- metallic foil
- vellum

embossing folders

Our Textured Impressions™ Embossing Folders have male (raised) and female (recessed) surfaces on opposite sides of a folder. When it is passed through a die-cutting or embossing machine, the folder applies pressure to cardstock to alter the surface, giving it a raised effect.

Molded plastic embossing folders do not cut paper. These folders only emboss and are designed to be used with a single sheet of thin material.

quilting/ appliqué

This exclusive collection of dies allows you to create personalized quilts and patchwork masterpieces, taking away the sometimes laborious task of using a ruler and rotary cutter. The collection features some of the most popular quilt shapes, including standard squares and triangles, as well as Apple Core, Dresden Plate, Drunkard's Path, and much more!

You can cut multiple layers of fabric at any one time with these hardy and versatile dies, giving you a precise and clean cut every time. They even come with a built-in 1/4 inch seam allowance to make piecing by hand or machine even easier!

Textured Impressions

Textured Impressions Embossing Folders offer the deepest and boldest embossing experience. You can turn ordinary cardstock, paper, metallic foil, or vellum into an embossed, textured master-piece. The large folder also fits the exact dimensions of an A2 or A6 card, while the small, medium, or border sizes create amazing embellishments.

Accessories

Our complete line of accessories will further enhance your creative life. Make creating easier with our Magnetic Platform, Stamper's Secret Weapon™, and Tool Kit. Embrace efficiency by using our Cut & Emboss Paper and Mat Board Packs. Expand your creative potential with Embossing Diffusers™ and the Dimensional Cutting Pad. And don't forget to keep your crafting tools organized with our Die & Embossing Storage!

System Comparison/Compatibility Chart

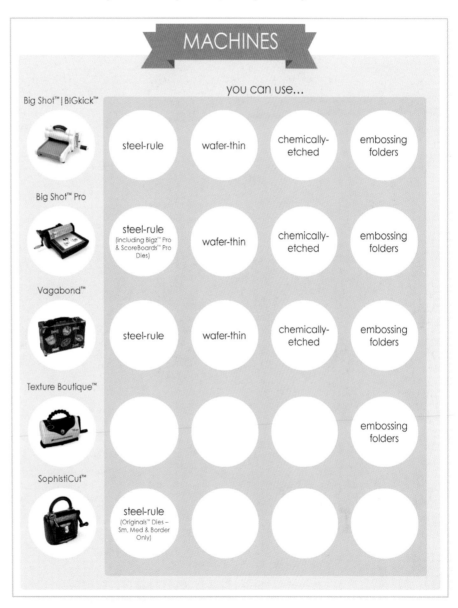

MACHINES

you can use...

	steel-rule	wafer-thin	chemically-etched	embossing folders
Big Shot™ | BIGkick™	steel-rule	wafer-thin	chemically-etched	embossing folders
Big Shot™ Pro	steel-rule (including Bigz™ Pro & ScoreBoards™ Pro Dies)	wafer-thin	chemically-etched	embossing folders
Vagabond™	steel-rule	wafer-thin	chemically-etched	embossing folders
Texture Boutique™				embossing folders
SophistiCut™	steel-rule (Originals™ Dies – Sm, Med & Border Only)			

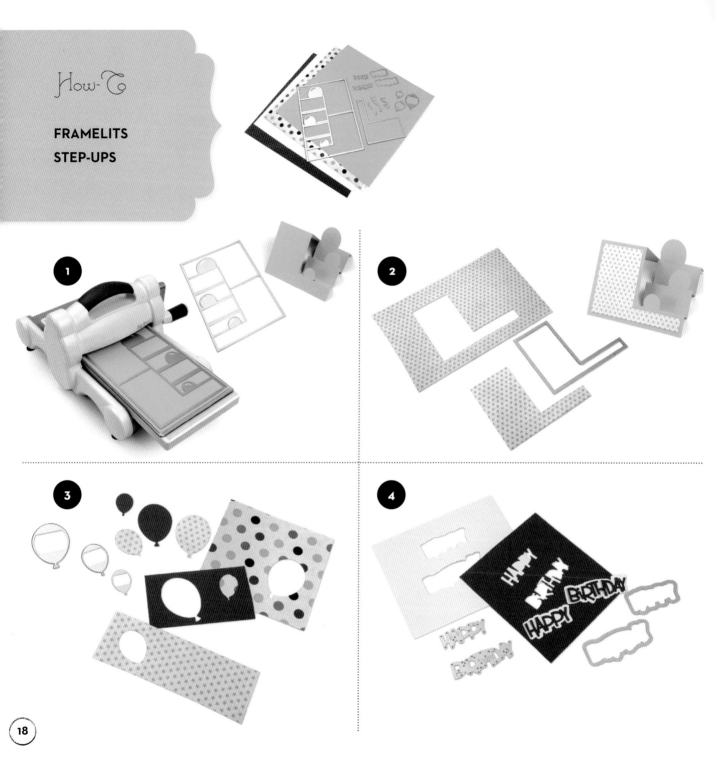

How-To

**FRAMELITS
STEP-UPS**

1

2

3

4

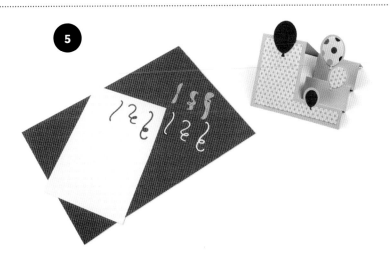

5

How-To

FRAMELITS ELEGANT STAND-UPS

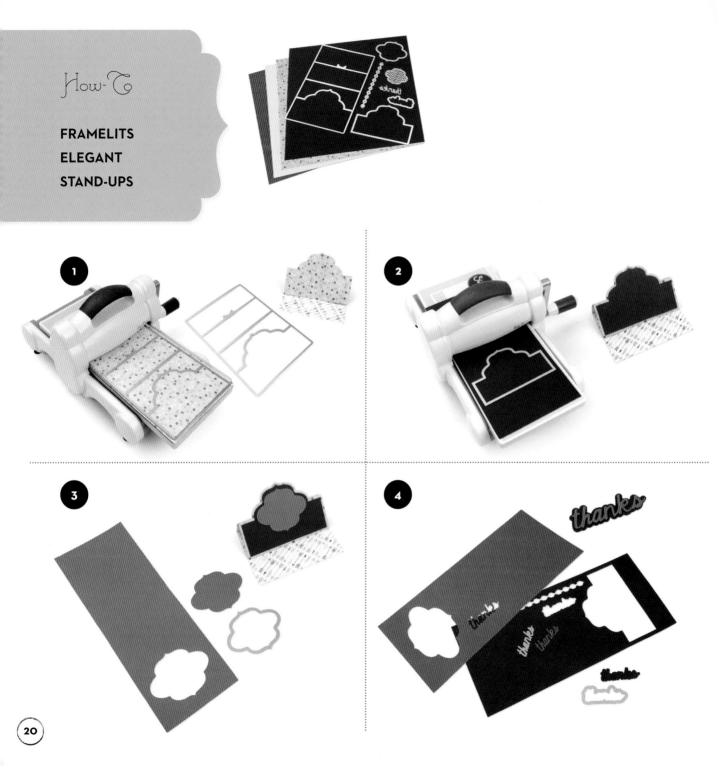

How-To

FRAMELITS
CIRCLE
FLIP-ITS

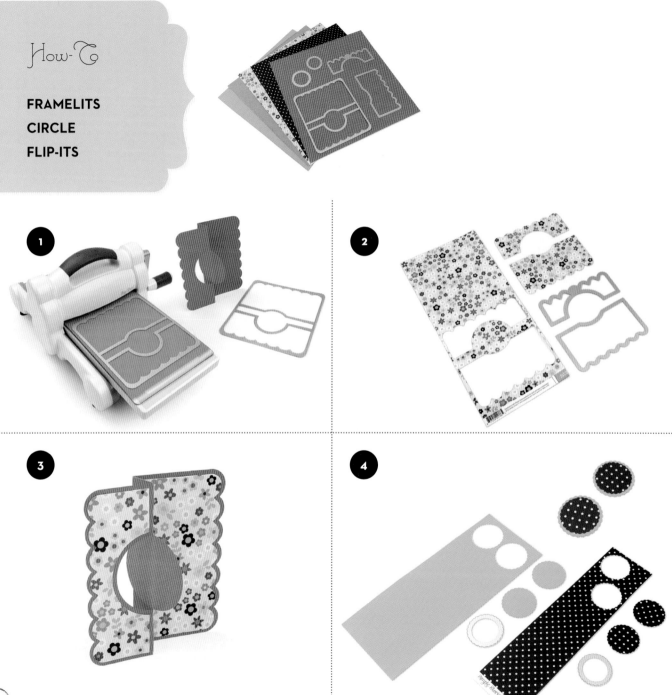

Celebrations

happy birthday

Birthday
Wishes

Butterfly Birthday Wishes

SUPPLIES:
Framelits: Card, Royal
Flip-its; Labels, Royal
Framelits w/Stamps:
Word Labels
Triplits: Butterfly

TIPS N' TRICKS:
Use 2 different designer
papers to decorate the
Flip-its Card.

For You with Pink Flowers

SUPPLIES:
Framelits: Labels, Royal
Framelits w/Stamps:
Flowers & Tags
Thinlits: Borders

For You

Happy Birthday
with Rick-Rack

SUPPLIES:
Framelits: Card,
Elegant Flip-its; Borders
The Stamps of Life:
elegant2stamp Set

HAPPY
BIRTHDAY!

Vroom Vroom

SUPPLIES:
Framelits: Card,
Elegant Flip-its
Framelits w/Stamps: Cars

vroom vroom

Happy Birthday

Stop

SUPPLIES:
Framelits: Card,
Regal Stand-Ups
Framelits w/Stamps: Windows

Happy Birthday Candle Card

SUPPLIES:
Framelits: Card,
Basic Step-Ups
The Stamps of Life:
candles4birthday;
Candle Dies

Happy Birthday Roses Cake

SUPPLIES:
Framelits: Card, Circle Flip-its #2
Framelits w/Stamps: Birthday Cake

TIPS N' TRICKS:
Stamp in a lighter shade and then carefully color images for a different look.

Regal Pink & Green Blooms

SUPPLIES:
Framelits: Card, Regal Stand-Ups
Framelits w/Stamps: Phrases
Thinlits: Borders **Triplits:** Flowers and Flowers #2

(Leaves from same sheet as Step-Ups Card)

TIPS N' TRICKS:
Use a ball tool to mold die cut Flowers into a foam block, giving a petal shape.

Butterfly Happy Birthday

SUPPLIES:
Framelits: Royal Flip-its
Triplits: Butterfly and Flower #2
Framelits w/Stamps: Cars

TIPS N' TRICKS:
Hang the butterfly off of the "flip" part of the card to add a different look. Cut flower from wool felt for a fantastic embellishment.

Happy Birthday Cake

SUPPLIES:
Framelits: Card,
Elegant Stand-Ups
Framelits w/Stamps:
Birthday Cake
Triplits: Flower

TIPS N' TRICKS:
To add different colors to stamped image, stamp it again onto patterned paper. Then cut part of it out, gluing it to the original image, as with the pink trim on the Cake Stand.

Happy Birthday with Purple & Blue Flower

SUPPLIES:
Framelits: Card, Regal Stand-Ups; Labels, Regal
Framelits w/Stamps: Circles & Tags
Triplits: Flower #2

Happy Birthday
Wish

SUPPLIES:
Framelits: Card, Regal
Stand-Ups; Labels, Regal
Framelits w/Stamps: Phrases

Happy Birthday Tag Card

SUPPLIES:
Framelits w/Stamps: Tags
Clear Stamps: Birthday

TIPS N' TRICKS:
Include different sentiments on the Tag.

happy **birthday**
you aren't getting older,
you're getting wiser!

SUPPLIES:
Framelits: Card, Regal
Stand-Ups; Labels, Regal
The Stamps of Life:
froggy2love Set
Froggy Dies

TIPS N' TRICKS:
Continue scene on base of
Stand-Ups Card.

Hoppy
Birthday!!!

Balloons in a Scalloped Circle

SUPPLIES:
Framelits: Card; Circle #4
Flip-its **Triplits:** Balloons
Clear Stamps: Birthday

TIPS N' TRICKS:
Hang the Balloon off the "flip" part of the card. Add a second Balloon on the backside of the Balloon so Balloons are back to back.

Happy Birthday with 3 Cars

SUPPLIES:
Framelits: Card, Triple Square Flip-its
Framelits w/Stamps: Cars
Thinlits: Borders

TIPS N' TRICKS:
Repeat design on Triple Square Flip-its Card for extra impact.

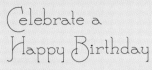

Celebrate a Happy Birthday

SUPPLIES:
Framelits: Card, Elegant
Stand-Ups; Card, Royal Flip-its
(Optional: Ribbon Sliders)
Framelits w/Stamps: Cars;
Birds & Tree; Phrases

TIPS N' TRICKS:
Ribbon Sliders, like those
in the Framelits Royal
Flip-its Card Set, add
great interest.

For You in Blue

SUPPLIES:
Triplits: Heaxagon
Framelits w/Stamps: Flowers & Tags

FOR YOU

Just for You
with a White Rose

SUPPLIES:
Framelits: Card, Regal Flip-its
The Stamps of Life:
stamps4fancylabel Set

Happy Birthday Ladybug

SUPPLIES:
Framelits: Labels, Regal
The Stamps of Life: ladybugs2love Set

TIPS N' TRICKS:
Use the Framelits Label Dies to create fun-shaped cards. Turn the Framelits Regal Labels one-eighth of a turn when layering onto card for a second design idea.

News Flash!

SUPPLIES:
Framelits: Card, Triple
Fancy Flip-its
The Stamps of Life:
tv2stamp Set

Happy Birthday with Polka-Dot Balloons

SUPPLIES:
Framelits: Card, Balloons Step-Ups

TIPS N' TRICKS:
Allow certain card elements to overhang card edges, but remember to make the envelope large enough.

Happy Birthday with Yellow Roses

SUPPLIES:
Framelits: Card,
Basic Step-Ups;
Card, Regal Stand-Ups

TIPS N' TRICKS:
Punch a hole in layered
Flowers and secure all layers
with a brad.

Happy Birthday Car & Balloons

SUPPLIES:
Framelits: Card, Royal Flip-its; Card, Balloons Step-Ups
Framelits w/Stamps: Cars; Phrases

TIPS N' TRICKS:
To add an interactive element, add twine to Balloon die-cuts.

Happy Birthday, My Friend

SUPPLIES:
Framelits: Card,
Basic Step-Ups; Labels, Royal
The Stamps of Life:
chalksayings2stamp Set;
Life Chalk Set

TIPS N' TRICKS:
Mix and match the Flowers
from the Framelits Basic
Step-Ups Card to decorate
your card.

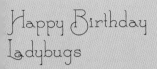

Happy Birthday Ladybugs

SUPPLIES:
Framelits: Card,
Basic Step-Ups; Labels, Regal
The Stamps of Life:
ladybugs2love Set;
Ladybugs

TIPS N' TRICKS:
Die cut 2 Flourishes using
different colored cards.
Overlap one color slightly
over the second color for
a two-tone effect.

Have a Sweet Day Card

SUPPLIES:
Framelits w/Stamps:
Ice Cream

TIPS N' TRICKS:
Tie a small bow, glue to card, add tiny paper flowers and button.

have a sweet day!

Cupcake Scallop

SUPPLIES:
Framelits: Card,
Circle Flip-its #4
Triplits: Cupcakes; Banner
Clear Stamps: Birthday

TIPS N' TRICKS:
To stamp a longer sentiment in a smaller space, make part of the sentiment and then stamp separately.

Happy Birthday with Pastel Balloons

SUPPLIES:
Framelits: Card, Balloons Step-Ups

TIPS N' TRICKS:
Use the accessory pieces in the Framelits Balloons Step-Ups Card to give your Balloons a different look.

Sweet Yellow Birthday Cake

SUPPLIES:
Framelits: Card, Elegant Stand-Ups; Labels, Fancy #4
Framelits w/Stamps: Birthday Cake

TIPS N' TRICKS:
Ink the edges of the die-cut for a layered look.

Happy Birthday with Pink Candles

SUPPLIES:
Framelits: Card, Elegant Stand-Ups; Labels, Elegant
The Stamps of Life: candles4birthday Set

Happy Birthday Chalkboard Style

SUPPLIES:
Triplits: Banner
The Stamps of Life:
birthday4cookie Set

TIPS N' TRICKS:
Use white pigment ink when stamping or writing on dark colors.

Button Lollipop

SUPPLIES:
Framelits: Labels, Fancy #6
The Stamps of Life: Merry & Bright Stamps

TIPS N' TRICKS:
Fold the cardstock in half and place on the inside of the die when cutting to form the card. Wrap a button in cellophane to create the lollipop.

PROJECT:
Glue and tie the tag to the front of a jar filled with old-fashioned lollipops, making it a more important part of the gift.

4 Birthday Tags

SUPPLIES:
Triplits: Tags
The Stamps of Life:
spinner2stamps Set

PROJECT:
Attach tags to bright colored
gift boxes that can later be used
as storage boxes.

Bring on the CAKE!

Open my present first!

Birthday wishes to you!

Enjoy your SPECIAL day!

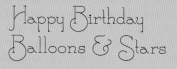

Happy Birthday Balloons & Stars

SUPPLIES:
Framelits: Card,
Royal Stand-Ups
Triplits: Balloons
Clear Stamps: Birthday

PROJECT:
Set your birthday buffet table with place cards that people can write their own names on to hold their place when they step away from the table to go for seconds!

Golden Gift

SUPPLIES:
Framelits: Card, Regal
Flip-its **Triplits:** Gift Die Set

TIPS N' TRICKS:
To add dimension, raise
different sections of the
"gift focal point" with
adhesive foam pads.

PROJECT:
A special card with an
individual sentiment placed
on each person's plate makes
the occasion even more
memorable.

A Cupcake for You

SUPPLIES:
Framelits: Card,
Charming Stand-Ups
Framelits: Card,
Triple Square Flip-its
Triplits: Cupcakes

TIPS N' TRICKS:
Use the border from the
Triple Square Flip-its Card Set
to edge both sides of the card.

PROJECT:
Birthday in bed—a nighttime
treat for an extraordinary
birthday girl with a note to tell
her how much you love her.

Happy Birthday for My Friend

SUPPLIES:
Framelits: Card, Triple Square Flip-its
Framelits w/Stamps: Friendly Phrases

TIPS N' TRICKS:
Use the border from the Triple Square Flip-its Card Set to edge both sides of the card.

PROJECT:
Make a card, write a personal message, and adhere it to the front of a photo album commemorating a special day.

Regal Love

SUPPLIES:
Framelits: Card, Regal Flip-its; Card, Regal Stand-Ups
Framelits w/Stamps: Birthday Cake
Triplits: Heart

TIPS N' TRICKS:
Use metallic embossing powder on stamped images for additional shimmer.

Red & Pink Butterflies for You

SUPPLIES:
Triplits: Butterfly
Framelits: Card,
Royal Stand-Ups

TIPS N' TRICKS:
Thread ribbon through
Border Die included in
Framelits Royal Stand-Ups
Card Set and add a bow.

Little
Black Dress

Love

SUPPLIES:
Framelits: Card, Charming
Frame Flip-its; Card,
Charming Stand-Ups

TIPS N' TRICKS:
Die cut 4 or 5 of the Love die
and layer together for a chipboard effect.

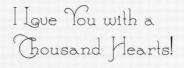

I Love You with a Thousand Hearts!

SUPPLIES:
Framelits: Card, Hearts
Step-Ups

TIPS N' TRICKS:
Use the Hearts from the Small Triple Heart die to add dimension to the heart border.

Boo Candy Corn

SUPPLIES:
Framelits: Card,
Fancy Frame Flip-its
The Stamps of Life:
candycorn2cut Set

Trick or Treat

SUPPLIES:
Framelits: Card,
Royal Stand-Ups
The Stamps of Life:
candycorn2cut Set

Just for You with Acorns

SUPPLIES:
Framelits: Card, Royal Stand-Ups; Labels, Royals
Triplits: Leaf

TIPS N' TRICKS:
Add dimensional lines to the top of the Acorn using a black marker.

SUPPLIES:
Triplits: Tags
Thinlits: Borders
Clear Stamps: Birthday

TIPS N' TRICKS:
Add rhinestones to the accessory pieces for holiday glitter!

Trees for Christmas

SUPPLIES:
Framelits: Card, Elegant
Stand-Ups; Labels, Elegant
The Stamps of Life:
trees4Christmas Set;
Tree Dies

TIPS N' TRICKS:
Create a Gatefold Card by
die cutting two Stand-Ups
Cards and joining the bases
to each other.

Peace, Love & Joy

SUPPLIES:
Framelits: Card,
Triple Circle Flip-its
The Stamps of Life:
trees4Christmas Set;
Tree Dies

TIPS N' TRICKS:
Leave the "flip" side of the
Triple Circles blank so you
can write your greeting.

Merry Christmas with Ornaments & Stars

SUPPLIES:
Framelits: Card, Elegant Stand-Ups
Triplits: Ornaments
Framelits w/Stamps: Tags

Merry Christmas

Merry Christmas with Gold Polka Dots

SUPPLIES:
Framelits: Card, Square Flip-its #2
Framelits w/Stamps: Tags
Triplits: Christmas Trees

3 Christmas Trees

SUPPLIES:
Framelits: Card,
Charming Stand-Ups
Framelits w/Stamps: Tags
Triplits: Christmas Trees

TIPS N' TRICKS:
Don't limit yourself to a
simple Stand-Ups card
design. Items can also
go above the card.

Christmas Ornament with Snowflakes

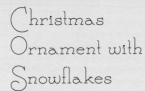

SUPPLIES:
Framelits: Card, Circle Flip-its #4
Framelits w/Stamps: Tags
Triplits: Ornaments

TIPS N' TRICKS:
Use the circles left over from center of Ornament and outer circle of snowflake to embellish card front.

Joy
Christmas Tree

SUPPLIES:
Framelits: Fancy Label
Triplits: Trees
The Stamps of Life:
moreornaments4Christmas
Stamp Set

Merry Christmas

Merry Christmas
Tag Card

SUPPLIES:
Framelits: Card,
Square Flip-its #2
Framelits w/Stamps: Tags
Triplits: Tags

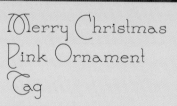

Merry Christmas Pink Ornament Tag

SUPPLIES:
Framelits w/Stamps: Tags
Triplits: Ornaments

TIPS N' TRICKS:

Die cut 4 or 5 pieces of the top Ornament and layer together on card for chipboard effect. Use the circles left over from the center of the Ornament and outer circle of snowflakes to embellish card.

Merry Christmas

Merry Christmas

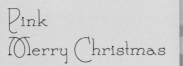

Pink
Merry Christmas

SUPPLIES:
Triplits: Christmas Trees
Framelits w/Stamps: Tags

TIPS N' TRICKS:
Use Tag for a personal
sentiment.

Baubles &
Snowflakes

SUPPLIES:
Framelits: Card, Elegant
Flip-its; Labels, Elegant; Card,
Regal Flip-its (*for the border*)
Framelits w/Stamps: Tags

TIPS N' TRICKS:
Layer Snowflake die cuts and
add adhesive gems to centers
for additional sparkle!

Merry Christmas with Triple Packages

SUPPLIES:
Triplits: Gifts
Framelits w/Stamps: Tags

TIPS N' TRICKS:
Use the same Gifts Die Set 2 or 3 times with different papers to create variation.

Merry Christmas

Dad

SUPPLIES:
Framelits: Card,
Royal Flip-its; Labels, Royal
The Stamps of Life:
all4dads Stamp Set

PROJECT:
A photo box filled with Dad's
favorite pictures is even more
of a keepsake with a card
adhered to the lid filled with
notes from his children.

The Family Car

SUPPLIES:
Framelits w/Stamps: Cars

TIPS N' TRICKS:
Use the largest die in the set to create this project.

PROJECT:
A photo box with the "emblem" of what is inside—this one, of course, is a family vacation across the country.

Happy Halloween with a Green Owl

SUPPLIES:

Framelits: Card, Circle Flip-its #4

Framelits w/Stamps: Autumn Owls

The Stamps of Life: owl2love Set

PROJECT:

This card is glued to the trick-or-treat container, making it part of the holiday decorations.

Triple Hoot Owls

SUPPLIES:
Framelits: Card,
Triple Fancy Frame Flip-its
The Stamps of Life:
owl2love Set

PROJECT:
An inspiration board should hold photos, cards, and memories of each holiday.

Candy Tin Tags

SUPPLIES:
Triplits: Tags

PROJECT:
Create individual Tags adhered to tins filled with candy, or office or art supplies. Tags can also be hung on the tree.

Merry Christmas
Sequin Ornaments

SUPPLIES:
Framelits: Labels, Fancy #4
Triplits: Ornaments
The Stamps of Life:
ornaments4Christmas Set

TIPS N' TRICKS:
Cut 2 Ornaments from cardstock, one from foam and one from plastic, to create the shaker Ornaments.

PROJECT:
Welcome people to your home for the holidays with a simple wreath with a card attached.

Merry Christmas

Sentiments

Thinking of You
In Yellow & Gray

SUPPLIES:
Framelits: Card,
Fancy Frame Flip-its #2;
Labels, Fancy #4
The Stamps of Life:
labels4cutting Set

Take Care

SUPPLIES:
Framelits: Card, Elegant Flip-its; Card, Elegant Stand-Ups; Labels, Elegant

Thanks So Much

SUPPLIES:
Framelits: Card, Square
Flip-its #2; Flower #2
Framelits w/Stamps:
Word Labels; Leaves

TIPS N' TRICKS:
Mix and match the Flower Dies
and papers to create flowers.

Thank You

SUPPLIES:
Framelits w/Stamps:
Flowers & Tags;
Framelits: Labels, Elegant
Textured Impressions
Embossing Folders:
Dotted Squares Set

TIPS N' TRICKS:
Emboss die-cut shapes to
give texture to your card.

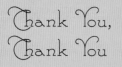

Thank You, Thank You

SUPPLIES:
Framelits: Card,
Square Flip-its #2; Squares
Framelits w/Stamps:
Thank You; Phrases

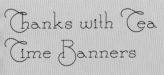

Thanks with Tea Time Banners

SUPPLIES:
Framelits: Card, Elegant Stand-Ups
Framelits w/Stamps: Teapot
Triplits: Banner

TIPS N' TRICKS:
Select decorative elements and raise them by using adhesive foam pads.

You're My Cup of Tea Teapot

SUPPLIES:
Framelits w/Stamps: Teapot; Flowers & Tags

TIPS N' TRICKS:
Create a shaped card by die cutting large Teapot twice. Score a line ½ inch (12 mm) down from top of the back card. Add tape and adhere to back of front card piece.

Use Petal Die from Flowers & Tags Set to create a hole for the handle.

You're My Cup of Tea

SUPPLIES:
Framelits: Card, Elegant Flip-its; Labels, Elegant
Framelits w/Stamps: Teapot; Birthday Cake

TIPS N' TRICKS:
Cut one Banner from Birthday Cake Set in half to make the smaller Banner Flags.

You're my cup of tea!

Life Is Good

SUPPLIES:
Triplits: Flowers

TIPS N' TRICKS:
Hand cut and fold banner strip, add handwritten words.

life is good

sweet

Sweet
Button Flowers

SUPPLIES:
Framelits: Card,
Royal Stand-Ups
Triplits: Flower #2

Royal Butterfly
Just for You

SUPPLIES:
Framelits: Card,
Royal Stand-Ups
Triplits: Butterfly; Flower
(Optional: Butterfly Trail)

TIPS N' TRICKS:
Use the Butterfly Trail Die for
decorative elements elsewhere
on the card.

Hello Butterflies

SUPPLIES:
Triplits: Butterfly
Framelits w/Stamps: Phrases

TIPS N' TRICKS:
For a quick card, purchase white cards to decorate.

You Mean the World To Me

SUPPLIES:
Framelits: Card, Elegant Stand-Ups
Framelits w/Stamps: Word Labels
Thinlits: Borders

Triplits: Leaf
Textured Impressions Embossing Folders: Dotted Square Set

TIPS N' TRICKS:
Use white embossing powder to make stamps stand out on dark cardstock.

you mean the world to me

Thinking of You

SUPPLIES:
Framelits w/Stamps:
Flowers & Tags

TIPS N' TRICKS:
Use vellum to stamp and
die cut Flowers.

THINKING OF YOU

Thanks!
Felt Flower

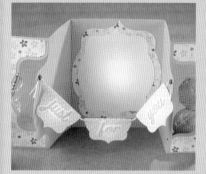

SUPPLIES:
Framelits: Card,
Royal Stand-Ups; Labels, Royal
Triplits: Flower
Framelits w/Stamps: Phrases

TIPS N' TRICKS:
Framelits die cut wool felt,
which can be found at certain
fabric stores or online.

Thanks So Much Flower

SUPPLIES:
Framelits: Card, Square
Flip-its #2
Framelits w/Stamps: Word
Labels; For You & Thank You

TIPS N' TRICKS:
Spray ink onto a coffee filter
and die cut Flowers to create a
unique look.

A Little Treat For Someone Awesome

SUPPLIES:
Framelits: Card, Circle
Flip-its #2 **Framelits w/**
Stamps: Ice Cream
The Stamps of Life:
chalksayings2stamp Set

a little treat

for someone sweet!

You are
'berry'
sweet.

You Are Berry
Sweet

SUPPLIES:
Framelits: Card, Triple Fancy
Frame Flip-its
Triplits: Flower #2

The Stamps of Life:
strawberries2stamp Set;
morestrawberries2stamp Set

TIPS N' TRICKS:
Leave the back of the "flip"
panel blank to make room for
a greeting.

So Sorry In Yellow & Gray

SUPPLIES:
Framelits: Card, Circle
Flip-its #4 **Thinlits:** Borders

TIPS N' TRICKS:
For card borders, add die cut
felt for a different texture.

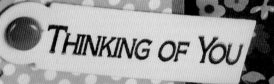

THINKING OF YOU

Thinking of You – Bee Happy

SUPPLIES:
Framelits: Card,
Circle Flip-its #2
Framelits w/Stamps:
Flower & Tags
Triplits: Bee

TIPS N' TRICKS:
Add a Tag at an angle on
your card.

You're My Sweet Rock Candy Tag

SUPPLIES:
Thinlits: Borders

TIPS N' TRICKS:
Cut patterned paper into a rectangle for an easy card.

Vroom Vroom with Blue Car

SUPPLIES:
Framelits: Card, Royal
Flip-its; Borders
Framelits w/Stamps: Cars

TIPS N' TRICKS:
Add different borders to each
side of the card.

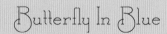

Butterfly In Blue

SUPPLIES:
Framelits: Card,
Royal Flip-its
Triplits: Butterfly

Royal Blooms

SUPPLIES:
Framelits: Card,
Royal Flip-its
Triplits: Flower; Flower #2

TIPS N' TRICKS:
Add vellum petals when
making layered Flowers for
a different look.

bloom

Thank You with Pink & Yellow Flowers

SUPPLIES:
Framelits: Card, Circle Flip-its #2
Framelits w/Stamps: Phrases **Triplits:** Flower #2

TIPS N' TRICKS:
Layer Triplits Flowers to create different flower combinations.

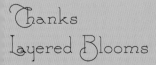

Thanks
Layered Blooms

SUPPLIES:
Textured Impressions
Embossing Folders: Dotted
Square Set **Triplits:** Flower;
Flower #2 **Framelits:** Card,
Elegant Stand-Ups

TIPS N' TRICKS:
Use an embossed background
layer for added interest.

Friend with
Birds

s:
s: Card, Royal Flip-its
s w/Stamps:
ree

TIPS N' TRICKS:
Attach a decorative image
to edge of the moving
Flip-its section so that the
image "floats" when you
open the card.

Miss You

SUPPLIES:
Framelits: Card,
Square Flip-its #2
Framelits w/Stamps:
Flowers & Tags
Triplits: Flower

TIPS N' TRICKS:
For added texture, use
Framelits to die cut
Flowers with wool felt.

you're so sweet

Got Candy?

SUPPLIES:
Framelits: Card, Regal Flip-its
The Stamps of Life:
candy2share Set

got candy?

Live, Love, Ladybug

SUPPLIES:
Framelits: Card, Royal Stand-Ups
Framelits w/Stamps: Flowers & Tags
Triplits: Butterfly
Thinlits: Border

The Stamps of Life:
ladybugs2love Set

TIPS N' TRICKS:
Use Border dies to create a background on card.

Bee You

SUPPLIES:
Framelits: Card, Square Flip-its #2; Labels, Fancy #4
Triplits: Bee; Flower
The Stamps of Life: hive4bees Set

Bee You

Thanks So Much with Bee

SUPPLIES:
Framelits: Card, Square Flip-its #2
Framelits w/Stamps: Word Labels
Triplits: Bee; Butterfly

You Deserve a Treat

SUPPLIES:
Framelits: Flip-its Circle #4
Framelits w/Stamps:
Ice Cream

TIPS N' TRICKS:
Have fun with sequins!
Paint white glue onto desired
areas and sprinkle on sequins.
A unique look will be created
each time!

you deserve a treat!

have a sweet day!

Thanks with Daisies

SUPPLIES:
Framelits: Card,
Elegant Stand-Ups

TIPS N' TRICKS:
Handwrite a fun sentiment
and add doodles with a pen.

thanks

Sending a little note

SUPPLIES:
Framelits: Labels, Royal
Framelits w/Stamps:
Ice Cream

have a
sweet day!

For You
In Pink & Black

SUPPLIES:
Framelits: Card,
Elegant Stand-Ups;
Labels, Elegant
Framelits w/Stamps:
Flowers & Tags

For You

thanks

THINKING OF YOU

SUPPLIES:
Framelits: Labels, Fancy #4
Framelits w/Stamps:
Flowers & Tags
Triplits: Butterfly

Thank You with Pink Pin-Dot Daisy

SUPPLIES:
Framelits w/Stamps:
Flowers & Tags;
Circles & Tags
Thinlits: Borders
Clear Stamps: Thanks

TIPS N' TRICKS:
Use Borders to divide card
and add a separated sentiment.

Just Buzzing By To Say Thanks

SUPPLIES:
Framelits: Card, Elegant Stand-Ups; Labels, Elegant
Triplits: Bee
The Stamps of Life: bee4me Set

TIPS N' TRICKS:
Use Bee #1 from the Bee Triplits Set to cut wings from glitter card. Insert this onto the wing area of the Bees.

Just buzzing by to say...

thanks

Hello My Friend

SUPPLIES:
Framelits: Card, Regal, Flip-its; Labels, Regal
Thinlits: Borders
The Stamps of Life: phone4you Set

TIPS N' TRICKS:
Turn the Framelits Die one-eighth of a turn when layering onto the center "flip" section for a different look.

Hello Hearts

SUPPLIES:
Framelits: Card,
Hearts Step-Ups
Framelits w/Stamps: Hello

TIPS N' TRICKS:
Stamp with vertical stamps
to fill in space differently.

Hello With Bees & Flowers

SUPPLIES:
Framelits w/Stamps: Windows

TIPS N' TRICKS:
Use both words and die-cut images to decorate in grid.

Hello Friend with Pink Roses

SUPPLIES:
Framelits: Card, Triple Circle Flip-its **Framelits w/Stamps:** Friendly Phrases

PROJECT:
Give a gift of a photo album filled with pictures of friends and a permanent card with a thought from each friend.

hello friend

Flowers Everywhere

SUPPLIES:
Framelits: Labels, Majestic #2;
Flower Layers & Leaf
Movers & Shapers L Die:
Card, Majestic Flip-its

TIPS N' TRICKS:
Use a Framelits die to cut
a window. Add acetate in
the window.

PROJECT:
A picnic basket is the perfect
gift—which means the tag
must be just as special.

Just for You

SUPPLIES:
Framelits: Card, Square
Flip-its #2;
Labels, Fancy #5
The Stamps of Life:
framefive2stamp Set;
Swirl Embossing Folder

TIPS N' TRICKS:
Emboss patterned paper with embossing folders to add texture.

PROJECT:
A notebook for a friend with a card glued to the front is much better than one that is just plain blue.

Hello My Friend

SUPPLIES:
Framelits: Card, Playful Flip-its; **Triplits:** Flowers, **Framelits w/Stamps:** Charming

PROJECT:
Frame your favorite photos and your favorite cards and hang them all together on the wall. Leave the glass off the card frame so that you can actually open the card.

Hugs
to you

Hugs to You

SUPPLIES:
Framelits: Hearts #2;
Hearts Scallop #2
The Stamps of Life:
dictionary4me Set;
sympathy4you Set

PROJECT:
Pictures and cards clipped
to small memo boards can
be hung around the room in
groups – much less expensive
than frames and easier to
update or change!